EVOLUTION OF THE HAWAIIAN ISLANDS

1 million years	STEP 1 -	Island formation over "Hotspot" (SEE PHOTOGRAPHS)
1-30 million years	STEP 2 -	Drift of the islands to the Northwest (3 inches/year) Erosion and subsidence
30 million years	STEP 3 -	Island submergence at the Darwin Point
70 million years	STEP 4 -	Subduction (Pacific seafloor sliding under the Asian continent)

North Pole

Mt. McKinley

Subduction

70

Mt. St. Helens

42

Seafloor Drift
(3 inches/year)

Mt. Fuji

JAPAN

30
Kure

NORTH
AMERICA

Darwin Point
(island submergence)

12

3

Hawaiian Islands

1 Isle
Formation

OCEANIC CRUST

Melting Anomaly
"Hotspot"

OUTER MANTLE

subduction
zone

INNER MANTLE

spreading
center

subduction
zone

CORE

EARTH IN CROSS SECTION

Richard Rhodes 3/31/88

HAWAIIAN HOTSPOT

Looking at a map of the Pacific Ocean, you may wonder why the Hawaiian Islands lie so far from any other landmass or island chain. Actually, the Hawaiian Islands lie at the southeastern tip of a line of seamounts, reef, and atolls that extends 4937 miles across the Pacific to the Aleutian Islands (just south of Alaska). The southern portion of this chain is called the Hawaiian Seamounts. Near Midway Island, the chain abruptly changes trend; these more northward-trending seamounts, named the Emperor Seamounts, appear to intersect with the Aleutian Trench.

The dating of these seamounts and islands indicates that the volcanoes were formed successively, with the oldest occurring near the Aleutian Trench and the youngest still forming south of the island of Hawai'i.

From the island of Hawai'i, the Hawaiian Ridge extends to the northwest as a strikingly linear feature. The ridge includes not only the well-known major islands from Hawai'i to Ni'ihau, but also banks, guyots, seamounts, and atolls. The major islands are large, high, and of obvious volcanic origin. They display a distinct age progression and progressive erosion. Hawai'i Island has peaks over 2.5 miles high and extensive lava fields that are almost undissected by erosion; by contrast, Kaua'i's spectacular scenery was carved by erosion so deep that we can tell that volcano has been extinct for several million years. Northwestward from Ni'ihau the remnants of the volcanic mountains projecting above sea level become

smaller and smaller. The last vestige of volcanic material is La Perouse Rock in French Frigate Shoals; from there to Kure Islands, the remnants of volcanoes are marked by atolls, each formed by coral growing up to the surface as the underlying volcano slowly subsides under its own weight and is eroded. Beyond Kure there are no further islands, but the chain of volcanoes is marked by guyots (drowned atolls) and seamounts. One by one the Hawaiian volcanoes grow, mature, and become extinct, to be replaced by new volcanoes to the southeast. The newest volcano, Lo'ihi, is only 36 miles south of Kilauea. It has grown to within 3,280 ft of the sea surface. In about 150,000 years, it will be the next Hawaiian island.

Why is the island chain linear? Why is there an age progression? The earth's surface is divided into a series of rocky plates moving relative to each other. Together, these plates form the "skin" or crust (the deeper lithosphere, and underlying material down to the earth's core, is termed the mantle). The ocean plates are formed by upwelling mantle material that extrudes at mid-ocean ridges and spreads laterally across the surface of the earth. Eventually the new crust cools and is pushed farther and farther from the spreading ridges. Eventually, after 100-200 million years, this ocean crust is consumed at subduction zones (which are associated with deep ocean trenches, island arcs, and explosive volcanism). With a return flow and reheating at depth, the plate tectonic machine acts as a giant convecting cell driven by the Earth's heat.

J.T. Wilson, in 1963, suggested that the Hawaiian Islands were formed as the Pacific

plate moved as described above and passes northwestward over a "hotspot" or melting anomaly deep within the mantle. The hotspot, which does not move, melts through the moving Pacific plate, thus forming the linear Hawaiian Island chain with its observed age progression. By 1972, this idea had been refined and developed by J. Morgan, who proposed that the Emperor Seamounts to the north of the Hawaiian chain were also formed by passage of the Pacific plate over the Hawaiian hotspot and thus were an extension of the Hawaiian Islands. Their different trend resulted from a change in the direction of the sea floor spreading, which created the Pacific seafloor about 40 million years ago.

Hotspots have now been identified all over the Earth, and they persist for several tens of millions of years (the Hawaiian hotspot has existed for at least 40 million years). They are the surface manifestation of a widespread planetary process that we do not completely understand—one that fascinates geologists, geophysicists, oceanographers, and planetary researchers alike. One thing is certain: Hawai'i, the most isolated hotspot and therefore the least contaminated by other effects, will always be of paramount importance as a geological laboratory. This volume is proof that scientists working in that laboratory, scientists who have been privileged enough to become familiar with Hawai'i's volcanoes, will continue to regard the volcanoes with awe and wonder.

GEOLOGY OF THE ISLAND OF HAWAI'I

The island of Hawai'i is the largest of the Hawaiian Islands. It consists of a number of coalesced volcanoes. The ages of these volcanoes range from approximately one half to three quarters of a million years to present. The locations of these volcanoes are shown in the adjoining satellite photograph. Kohala, on the north, is the oldest volcano. A second slightly younger volcano formed due south of Kohala and has been named Ninole volcano. This volcano ceased activity approximately 100,000 years ago and has been heavily incised by erosion. Subsequently, Mauna Kea and Mauna Loa volcanoes have grown between the two; Mauna Loa, in fact, has buried much of the Ninole volcano, and lavas from Mauna Kea bury part of and lap onto the flanks of Kohala volcano.

Right- A LANDSAT satellite image of the island of Hawaii shows the location of five volcanoes. Kohala, the oldest, forms the peninsula at the upper left of the island. Just south of Kohala, at the center and left margin of the photo, is Hualalai. Mauna Kea, seen at the center of the photo is volumetrically the smaller of the two central volcanoes. Mauna Loa is to the south and is larger in volume, although Mauna Kea is slightly higher. Kilauea is just to the east (to the right in this photograph) of Mauna Loa.

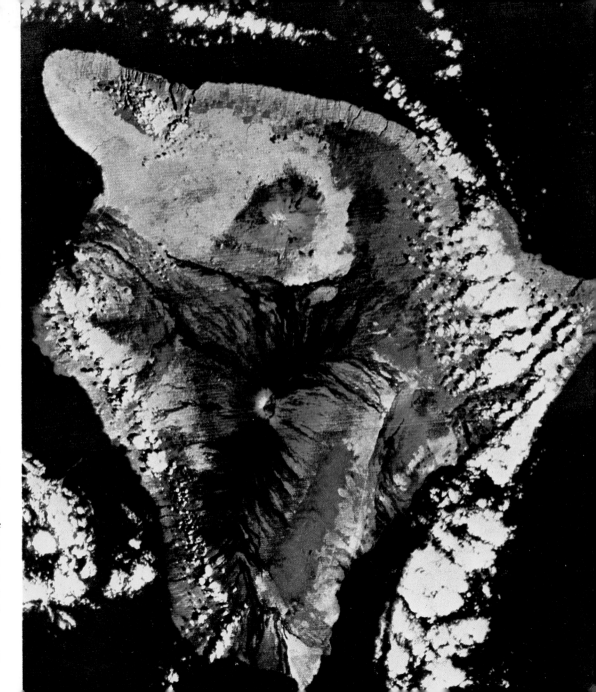

Rocks as old as 400,000 years from the Mauna Kea volcano have been dated by radiometric techniques. The top of Mauna Kea was glaciated during the ice age (approximately 15,000 years ago). At least three flows occurred after glaciation. No Hawaiian legends of volcanic activity are associated with Mauna Kea, and Macdonald and Abbott (1970) suggest that it was probably last active about 2,000 years ago. Earthquakes still occur occasionally under the mountain.

The Kulani Cone and Pu'u Lala'au stand near the summit of an eastern shield volcano that probably was formed at the same time as Mauna Loa. The late stages of volcanism of this volcano appear to have been quite explosive, since the Kulani and Pu'u Lala'au cones are large tephra (ejecta) cones. Today Kulani is almost entirely buried by Mauna Loa flows.

Hualalai, on the west side of the island, last erupted in 1800-1801. The geochemistry of the volcanic rocks suggests that it is intermediate in age and evolution between Mauna Kea and Mauna Loa. In 1929, several thousands of earthquakes occurred below the northern flank of the volcano. Thus, it is likely that Hualalai may now erupt every few hundred years.

Left- White patches of snow are seen on the lava flow of Moku'aweoweo crater on Mauna Loa. The summit crater is immense when compared to Kilauea. The cones within the summit crater were formed by activity in 1940 and 1949.

4

Mauna Loa volcano is large; however, many of its flows overlie the Ninole, Kulani, and Hualalai volcanoes. Regardless, Mauna Loa is probably the largest volcano on earth. Macdonald and Abbott (1970) estimated its volume as 10,000 cubic miles! By using the observed volcanic extrusion rate, we can deduce that the entire volcano could have been built from the sea floor in little more than one million years. Mauna Loa rises to 13,677 feet above sea level, and Mauna Kea reaches 13,796 feet. When measured from the base, Mauna Kea is the tallest mountain in the world, approximately 37,000 feet high.

Kilauea is the most active of the Hawaiian volcanoes. It is situated on the southeastern flank of Mauna Loa and abuts against the Kulani shield at depth. Scientists have debated whether the activity at Kilauea is influenced by Mauna Loa, as there have been several instances when the level of the lava lake at Halema'uma'u Crater (Kilauea) has dropped coincident with Mauna Loa eruptions. Additionally, eruptions have occurred nearly simul-

Above- The summit of Mauna Loa is seen in this photograph. Despite its gentle slopes this is one of the world's largest mountains. It is over 37,000 feet high (only a small portion of it is visible above sea level).

taneously on both volcanoes during 1868 and 1984. Work by J.G. Moore (cited by Macdonald and Abbott, 1970), further pointed out that the average rate of lava production for

southern Hawaii has been roughly the same over a long interval despite the fact that the activity was concentrated on Mauna Loa from 1934 to 1950 and subsequently on Kilauea. Geochemical studies suggest that lavas from the two volcanoes have reached slightly different stages of evolution. Thus, it would appear that the two volcanoes are fed by different magma bodies at depth. The large difference in elevation of the two eruptive centers 13,000 feet vs. 4,000 feet above sea level also suggests that the two do not have a common magma chamber at shallow depth. Recent seismic studies suggest that two separate conduits are observable at least to a depth of seven miles, but whether they remain separate at greater depth remains in question.

Left- An aerial photograph of the slopes of Mauna Loa show just how active it is. The geologically recent black lava flows cover older, weathered flows. It is obvious that much of the area on the slopes of Mauna Loa has been covered by young lava flows. An active lava stream can be seen at the top of the photograph. A series of collapse features can be seen at the bottom of the photograph which mark the position of an old lava tube.

MAUNA LOA

Mauna Loa is one of the largest volcanoes on Earth. It rises more than 13,000 feet above sea level, but the portion that is visible is like the tip of an iceberg; it is only a small part of the whole, which rises more than 30,000 feet above the deep Pacific Ocean floor. Although one of the highest mountains of Earth from its submerged base to is tip, Mauna Loa cannot be described as impressive; it is no stately cone like Mt. Fuji in Japan or Mayon in the Philippines, no snow-capped giant like Rainier in Washington state. Its gentle slopes and smooth outlines make it indeed a quite unimpressive and at first glance uninteresting mound. A true concept of its size may perhaps only be gained by ascending it. There are few trails to the summit, and the shortest and most convenient one begins at the 11,000-foot elevation on the northeast side. Here is situated a weather observatory, and it is possible to drive on a paved road all the way to the observatory from Hilo. On the map the observatory appears only three miles from the summit, seemingly a short and leisurely one-hour stroll. In reality the ascent is somewhat demoralizing because, with the uniform slope, the summit always appears to be only a few hundreds of yards ahead. The trail itself is over bare and often loose rock, with no vegetation or soil to cushion the feet. Above 10,000

Right- Molten rock splashes out of a channel near the Mauna Loa vent.

feet, moreover, many people feel the effects of altitude; for some this is merely a shortness of breath, but for a few it is altitude sickness. The three-mile hike takes well over three hours.

The foregoing should not be construed to mean that the ascent of Mauna Loa is not worthwhile. The scenery at the top is superb. For one thing, the air is clear. Mauna Loa projects well above the moist and cloudy air of the trade winds, and its summit is in bright sunshine most of the year except when an occasional tropical storm sweeps in and coats the mountain with snow. This clear air explains why Mauna Loa's dormant neighbor-volcano, Mauna Kea, has a cluster of astronomical observatories on its top. For another thing, there is the wild breathtaking beauty of Mauna Loa itself.

The slopes of Mauna Loa, though rocky, are never craggy, but spectacular craggy scenery does dominate the top. A great cliff-lined depression, three to four miles across, occurs at the top. This depression, known as Moku'aweoweo, is a volcanic caldera where the top of the volcano collapsed and subsided into itself. The observer on the rim of Moku'aweoweo may imagine a contest between destructive and constructive volcanic processes. Destructive processes have given rise to Moku'aweoweo and also several nearby smaller but most impressive chasms called pit craters. Constructive processes consist of the eruptions of lava flows that from time to time have flooded the floor of Moku'aweoweo, partially filled pit craters, and constructed small cinder cones. The contest is a slow one, and

the outcome may not be decided for millenia to come.

On Mauna Kea, a volcano that has reached its dormant stage, the outcome has already been decided: the constructive processes have won. Mauna Kea's summit caldera became completely buried, so completely that we cannot even be certain that it previously existed. The upward slope of the volcano continues right to the summit, where the broad main cone is diversified by smaller cinder cones heaped up in the latest eruptions.

The National Park Service maintains a small hut on the rim of Moku'aweoweo where, by arrangement, hikers may spend the night. It is furnished in a spartan way, with bunk beds for about twelve people and small room that can be used as a kitchen. Water is a problem, because rain does not fall often, and the porous volcanic rocks rapidly absorb what does fall. There is, however, a small waterhole near the hut containing either water or ice. Because of the severe climate, the entire upper 3,000 feet of Mauna Loa is a barren desert. Visitors must search carefully to find even the smallest vestige of plant life.

When visited and first surveyed in 1841 Moku'aweoweo was a coalescing group of two or three calderas and the floor of the middle one lay 900 feet below the summit. Now the subdivision is no longer apparent, because lavas levelled inequalities in the floor, which now lies 600 feet below the summit. Lua Poholo, an impressively deep pit crater at the northeast end of the caldera, skirted by the trail to the cabin, was not present in 1841,

demonstrating that the processes operating in the past 140 years have not been entirely constructive.

Most of the time Mauna Loa is peaceful, and a few wisps of steam emerging from cracks are the only reminder that the volcano is hot below the surface. The staff of the Hawaiian Volcano Observatory maintain a careful watch on the volcano—less careful than on Kilauea because of the difficult terrain, but very careful nonetheless. Several seismometers continuously transmit information by radio to the observatory, and ground deformation is measured periodically by observers who visit the summit region. The width of Moku'aweoweo, for example, is measured several times per year from rim to rim by high-precision laser devices, and the measurable width is known to increase before eruptions. These various measurements made it clear by mid-1983 that Mauna Loa would awaken and erupt within one or two years. The eruption came a bit sooner than expected, in March 1984, with only 11 hours of direct warning that an eruption was imminent.

Just how reliable are predictions of Mauna Loa's eruptions, and what are the factors that determine when an eruption occurs? Mauna Loa may be classed as a "steady state" volcano. When a graph is plotted of total lava emitted against time, a stepped line is obtained—each step represents one eruption—that approximates a straight line. This suggests that magma rises at a steady rate, amounting to about one cubic meter (nearly three tons) per second into the volcano from its source region 40 miles deep in the mantle. The magma then

PELE

It is difficult to live in Hawai'i without knowing several legends about Madame Pele. Unlike some other deities of ancient Hawai'i, Pele's stories are still told. Perhaps these legends live on because of the recurrent volcanic activity. If so, they may never die. In other volcanic islands of the Pacific similar stories are told; it is likely that the tradition of the volcano goddess was brought to Hawai'i by ancient Polynesian settlers. In fact, the ancient Hawaiian legends tell of Pele moving to Hawai'i from another land and supplanting a lesser volcano god. According to legends, Pele moved first to Kaua'i, then successively to O'ahu, Moloka'i, Lana'i, Kaho'olawe, Maui, and finally Hawai'i. Pele's home is said to be the firepit of Halema'uma'u crater. The word halema'uma'u means "house of ferns", and oral history records that long before Europeans came to Hawaii there were two pits inside Kilauea. One, like the present crater, was free of vegetation, while the other was much older and full of ama'uma'u ferns. Thus the name Halema'uma'u is derived from that older pit, now gone, and is an ancient one. Today, two stories of Madame Pele remain prominent in everyday Hawaiian life. First, when visiting Pele's home, the volcano, it is bad luck to eat any of the abundant berries of the 'ohelo plant without first tossing some to Pele. The second tradition is that one must be very respectful of any old women seen walking near the seacoast. The legends tell that Pele takes various forms, the most common being those of a beautiful golden-haired young woman or a very old woman walking along a lonely stretch of road. Legend has it that when Pele appears as an old woman, an eruption will occur soon—one that will make its way to the seacoast. Angry, bad-tempered, and jealous are words often used to describe Pele. According to legend, Pele is angered by many things: a lost or unfaithful lover, jealousy toward her sisters, failure in a sporting contest, or simply denial of something or someone desired. She easily loses her temper and stamps her feet, making the earth quake and break open in volcanic eruption. Legends tell of Pele weeping and tearing her hair, actions which, according to legend, account for the "Pele's hair" and "Pele's tears" often seen during volcanic eruptions. Pele's hair is spun glass that forms as hot lava and is thrown into the air during fountaining. Often as the ejecta cools from its liquid state, a thin strand of lava travels through the air and cools to form a fragile, thread-like piece of glass. The Pele's hair from the Kilauea eruption was golden in color. Pele's tears are actual tear-shaped drops of volcanic glass cooled in the air after being ejected from the volcano. They are most often black.

Right- Photographer Charles Myers of the Hawaii Institute of Geophysics made this photo montage of Pele rising from the crater of Kilauea. Images of human forms are frequently recognizable in the swirling smog above vents.

accumulates in a kind of holding chamber high inside the volcano, and when enough of it has accumulated it breaks through the rocks and is released at the surface. In the period 1830 to 1950 the interval between eruptions varied from 1 to 11 years and averaged 3-1/2 years. In the same period the interval between major eruptions characterized by large-volume outpourings from rift zones varied from 1 to 12 years and averaged 7-1/2 years. Because of the unequal times between its eruptions, the volcano departs from true steady-state conditions. The best explanation is that sometimes after an eruption the crack does not have time to heal before more magma rises from the holding chamber and another eruption ensues closely following the first. When the crack fully heals, by the solidifying of all the lava in it, it takes a full 8 to 12 years for enough magma to accumulate to make the next breakthrough.

There is thus a randomness in volcanic eruptions. From experience of a volcano's past record it is possible to judge at which stage in the inflation of a volcano (accumulation of magma causes a measurable uplift and a measurable widening of a caldera) the breakthrough is likely to occur. Once the magma begins to break through, a swarm of earthquakes

Left- During the initial outbreak of Mauna Loa lavas, the fountaining created a curtain of fire. As the eruption progressed, the fountaining became localized and built high spatter ramparts around the vents.

10

develops which informs the observers that an eruption is likely to happen within hours or days. In March 1984, it apparently took the magma only 1-1/2 hours to break through to the surface.

Since the 1950 eruption, Mauna Loa has changed its behavior and has apparently departed from the steady-state conditions of 1830 to 1950. Apart from the small eruption of 1975, a 34-year period of inactivity ensued which was unprecedented in Mauna Loa's historic record. By 1983 some people were wondering if the volcano had become dormant. The 1984 eruption has demonstrated that it is not dormant. Nevertheless there are reasons to suspect that a lower magma supply rate from the deep mantle source may have been operating since 1950. Only the future record will reveal whether or not this is so.

Eruptions of Mauna Loa almost always begin in the summit area. A fissure opens across or near Moku'aweoweo, and highly fluid lava spurts out along its whole length. This summit eruption reflects the fact that prior to an eruption the holding chamber in which magma accumulates is situated directly beneath the caldera. When enough magma has accumulated, or when that magma is in the appropriate physical condition, up it comes and breaks surface.

Moku'aweoweo is situated on a well-defined zone of ground cracking, one branch trending southwest from the caldera (the southwest rift zone) and the other trending east-northeast (the northeast rift zone). When a summit eruption occurs, cracks often extend laterally

Above- This electrical power line was toppled by the Mauna Loa flow near Kulani Correctional Facility. When this power line became threatened, the electrical power was rerouted to prevent a major disruption of power. Power from portable generators supplied the Mauna Loa Observatory. This observatory was scheduled to receive transmissions from the Solar Maximum Mission Satellite which was repaired in orbit by space shuttle astronauts.

into one or another of the rift zones some hours or days later, and the eruption then migrates from the summit area into a rift zone. Which rift zone becomes active seems to be determined by some random choice, as with the toss of a coin. In 1950 it was the southwest rift; in 1984 it was the northeast rift. Evidently magma can move equally easily into the higher part of each rift zone, but lower, the southwest rift is the weakest, and ground cracking permitting the eruption of lava may extend more or less down the entire flank of the rift to the coast. In 1950 rifting extended nearly halfway down to the coast, to as far as the 8,000 foot level; in 1907 it extended down to 6,000 feet and in 1868 to below 3,000 feet. The northeast rift, on the other hand, is more confined; the great mass of Mauna Kea to the north, and the smaller but still large mass of Kilauea to the south, buttress the eastern part of Mauna Loa's northeast rift and inhibit ground cracking low down on the rift; in consequence few eruptive fissures extend lower than the 9,000 foot level.

This inhibition of rifting into lower parts of Mauna Loa's northeast rift is fortunate for Hilo. This city of 40,000 people lies directly in the path of lavas from the northeast rift. The higher up in the rift that lavas erupt, the less likely that lava will extend into the town. In the first several days of the 1984 eruption,

Left- Forest fires are a formidable natural hazard created by volcanic eruptions. The lava flow from the Mauna Loa eruption burned the rain forest as it moved downhill.

lava headed rapidly toward Hilo and covered 15 of the 20 miles from the vent to the edge of town. The people, many of them knowing that lava had in 1881 entered what is now the outskirts of Hilo, had a worrisome time being advised as they were in frequent radio newscasts to prioritize their possessions in the event that evacuation became necessary. They were uncomfortably aware of the angry red glow seen at night upslope of the town. Fortunately the lava snaking its way through the forest stopped after 22 suspenseful days, and it became clear that Hilo was no longer in any danger.

Some of Mauna Loa's lava flows are among the longest known on Earth. Very long lava flows result when the discharge of lava from the vent is considerable, amounting to hundreds or thousands of cubic yards per second and sustained for days or weeks. Because of the relatively uniform ground shape, the resulting lava stream is narrow and far-reaching. The lava of 1859 originating far up on the northwest flank of Mauna Loa-where there is a trace of a third rift zone. The lava traveled northwestward some 34 miles and entered the sea

Right- These two men enjoy the heat. Volcanologist George Walker, of the University of Hawaii, in the yellow jacket, has studied more than thirty volcanoes around the world during his distinguished career. Charles Helsley, right, is director of the Hawaii Institute of Geophysics at the University's Manoa campus. The Institute, active in teaching and research in the earth and planetary sciences, employs approximately 300 people. Portions of this picture appear to be out of focus this is caused by the intense heat waves generated from the extremely hot rock.

near Kiholo. Perhaps it would have traveled 50 miles if the sea had not been there. Lavas of 1852, 1855, and 1881 originated from the same zone as the 1984 lava and traveled about 30 miles. In some of these long lava flows, like that of 1984, the flow of lava is confined to an open channel, whereas in others (the 1881 lava, for example) flow is confined to tubes under the surface crust. The famous Kaumana Cave in Hilo, which can be followed underground for more than a mile, is a splendid example of a tube and is accessible because the fluid lava drained out from it at the end of the eruption. Lava flowing in tubes has the potential to travel farther because it loses heat less rapidly than from an open channel.

What is the probability that a future lava flow will enter Hilo? From a geological perspective it seems almost inevitable that this will happen some day. Hilo is a fast-expanding city, and in a sense, the larger the city grows by building up on the slopes of Mauna Loa the greater is the risk. All over the world, with the increase in population and the resulting pressure on land, more and more people are coming to live close to volcanoes; this problem of increased volcanic risk is common to Japan, Indonesia, Italy, and all countries that have active volcanoes.

In the likely event that a lava flow enters Hilo, what then? Almost certainly it will present no hazard to life. Although near its vent a lava may flow faster than a person can run, by the time it has traveled 20 or 30 miles downslope the advancing flow-front has cooled considerably and generally moves at a moder-

ate to slow pace, giving plenty of time for people to escape. It will, however, destroy property. A likely scenario is that a 300-yard-wide lava flow will plow across the town, its direction determined by the slope of the land, and perhaps eventually reach the sea.

What can be done to prevent a flow entering Hilo? There are two options. One is to exploit a natural "safety valve" to lessen the flow of lava. The other is to take active steps to divert or slow down the advancing lava flow front. Let us consider each of these options.

Operation of the natural "safety valve" is exemplified by the lava which, in the first week of the 1984 eruption, moved steadily and strongly toward Hilo. The lava flow front was continuously fed from fresh lava delivered freely from the vent by a continuous open lava channel. Below about 10 miles downslope the flow slowed considerably partly by having to pass through forest and partly because of cooling, and a congested zone developed where fresh lava from above piled up against the slower-moving lava in front of it. The congestion was reminiscent of that in the great Roman army 2,000 years ago attacking a narrow bridge held by a few brave defenders, a congestion recorded by the poet in the lines "Those behind cried *forward*, and those in front cried *back*." The congested 1984 lava did the only thing possible—it broke out laterally to begin a new lava flow. This new lava flowed parallel with the first, which had by then more or less halted. The second lava reached about the same distance from the vent as the first, and then in turn halted when a second lateral

breakout occurred. Plans have been formulated for bombing or shelling the sides of a flow so as to promote lateral breakouts where they do not develop naturally, but these measures have not yet had to be employed on Hawai'i. The side of a lava flow on Etna was dynamited in 1983—the dynamite was exploded in holes drilled in the solid side of the lava stream–in an attempt to divert it, but the results were not proved because the flow was naturally diverted at about the time of detonation. In the 1669 eruption of the same volcano it is recorded that brave villagers, protected from the heat by hides, did succeed in breaching the side of a lava levee and diverting its flow.

The other option is to divert a lava by building barriers across its path or by cooling its flow-front with water. A barrier was successful on Etna in 1983, and a great quantity of pumped water was apparently successful in stopping a lava advancing on a town in Iceland in 1973. There is little doubt about the general value of these active measures to protect property.

Right- A moving lava flow can be seen through the collapsed roof of a lava tube during the eruption of Mauna Loa. As the flow moved downslope it broke out of this lava tube and remained on the surface.

Mauna Loa Eruption From the Air

One of the first geologists from the University of Hawai'i to see the Mauna Loa eruption was volcanology graduate student, Mary Caress, who was visiting the island of Hawai'i with relatives during the spring break from her classes at Manoa.

Purely by chance, Mary mentioned to the agent at the car rental office that she was a volcanology student and hoped to drive up and see the volcanoes. Early the next morning, the agent learned of the eruption and called Mary at her hotel to tell her. As a result, Mary gathered her gear and went to the nearest helicopter service, where she managed to get an early morning flight to see the eruption.

Many other people followed a different route and flew over the eruption in small planes direct from O'ahu or Hilo. On the flight from O'ahu, the first sight of activity was often the volcanic ash cloud. Patty Fryer, a geologist at the University, describes the scene as follows:

"By the time we were south of Moloka'i and had finished our ascent to 10,000 feet, we no-

Left- The line of smoking cinder cones (upper right) are the source of the Mauna Loa eruption. The lava flow pouring from the main cone is diverted around small islands of old lava. Observations at the flows suggest that these islands are not eroded by the flowing lava, rather, spectacular standing waves are often created as new lava contacts the barrier and flows around it.

THE STATEHOOD ERUPTIONS

In 1984, Hawaii celebrated its 25th anniversary as the fiftieth state to join the United States of America. How appropriate that Mauna Loa and Kilauea should provide simultaneous eruptions and fireworks for this celebration! The following pages show views of the two volcanoes from the air as well as the ground. The spectacular photographs were provided by students and faculty of the Geology and Geophysics, Meteorology, and Oceanography departments at the University of Hawaii, personnel from the Hawaii Institute of Geophysics and Institute of Astronomy, as well as interested individuals and former students.

This volume was compiled in order to share our studies of the volcano, as so few people were permitted to observe both the volcanoes firsthand.

ticed a peculiar cumulus cloud far to the southeast. The maximum elevation of the regional cloud cover was about 11,000 or 12,000 feet. The cloud we saw in the southeast was well above that. We estimated 15,000 feet. It was a strange color, by comparison with the snowy white clouds we were flying through. It was a pale yellowish tan, darker at its base. We suspected it was a gas cloud from the eruption. As we drew near the Big Island, the general cloud cover appeared to have increased and our hopes of being able to see the eruption site on our first pass dwindled. The cloud we had been watching for an hour grew nearer and dominated the sky as we flew toward Mauna Loa's northeast rift. Over the saddle between Mauna Loa and Mauna Kea, the cloud cover seemed spotty. We caught a glimpse of the saddle road beneath us and then, off to the left, ground smoke and our first glimpse of the toe of the active lava flow."

Most fly-over passengers were fortunate to get some views of the eruption by flying around the clouds. Fryer reports: "We banked right and almost immediately were just south of the apex of the northeast rift zone. As if someone had lifted the lid off the main course platter at Christmas dinner, we saw in rapid succession the main channel of the northernmost flow, the line of vents with thin fountains of spatter about 60 feet high, and a series of cracks about one mile long uphill from the vents that were producing great amounts of fumes. We were flying at about 11,000 feet at that point. Our pilot banked to the left and dropped our altitude to about 10,000 feet. Then he flew up the rift zone to give us a view of the lava channels in the flow and the three main vents producing the fountaining."

"The clouds that had given us concern for our ability to see the eruption at all were absent on the south side of the apex of the rift zone. We had a good view of the vents and the lava channels. There were five channels, three from the vent at the lowest elevation, one from the center vent and one, the largest, from the vent farthest up along the rift. Our next pass took us directly over the largest of the lava channels, the one emanating from the vent at the highest elevation. We were about 500 feet above the channel and could see large blocks of dark, cooler solidified material rafting along the flow surface. The speed of the flow was staggering, we estimated its advance at between 30 and 50 mph. The width of the large channel was quite variable downstream but must have been a good 164 feet at the vent."

"The three active vents were about 328 feet apart along the rift zone. Each had a different shape. The largest vent situated at the highest elevation built a spatter rampart about 100 feet high; it was breached to the north and the vent diameter was about the width of the lava channel emanating from it. The second vent, farther downslope, was also about 98 feet high. It had a central vent diameter of about

Preceding page- Daylight photographs of the Mauna Loa vents taken on April 1, 1984 show that they at first were encircled by small spatter cones. As the eruption continued the spatter cones coalesced to form ramparts.

Right- The Mauna Loa flow can take on different appearances. In the left photograph, the flow looks like a satiny golden ribbon on black velvet. The photograph at right appears to be an articulate branching flow reminiscent of coral trees.

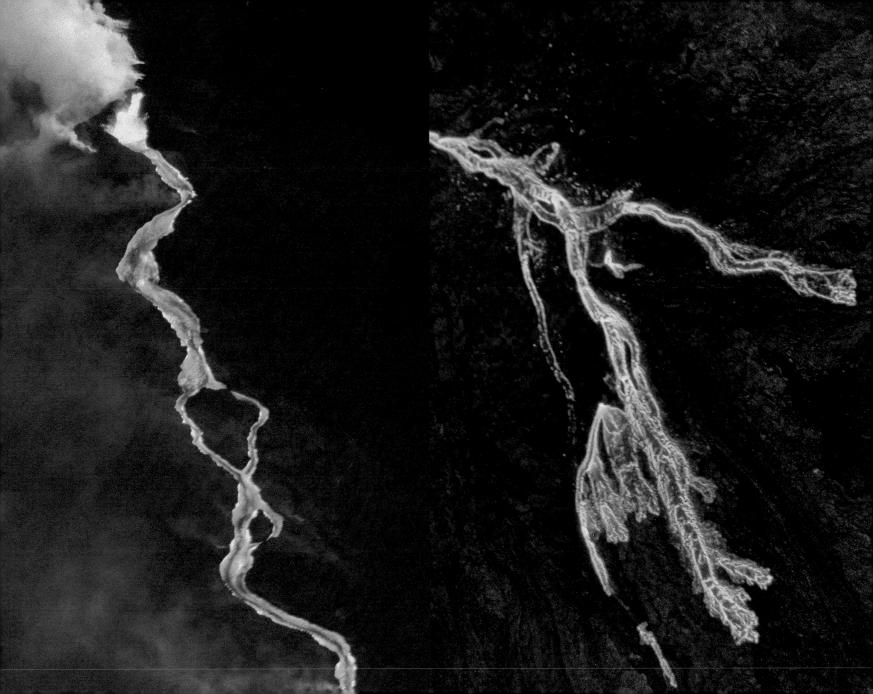

66 feet and was partially breached to the northeast. A lava channel about 66 feet wide at the vent but rapidly expanding to about 98 feet flowed northeast out of the vent. The third vent, the one situated furthest downslope along the rift zone, was probably a composite vent. The spatter rampart around the third vent was a few feet lower than those around the other two. The cone was breached to the north and

lavas flowed out from the vent toward the north and northeast in an intricately braided series of flows with three main channels."

"After four passes over the vents we left the site and flew back over the lower elevations of the rift zone. As we departed we were closer to Hilo than when we had approached the eruption site. We could see the distal edges of the flow and the smoke in the 'ohi'a forest. At the angle from which we were looking, the white structures on the outskirts of Hilo appeared ominously close to the edges of the flow. Our sympathy for the fears of the residents mixed with our excitement at having just witnessed such a spectacular display of the Earth's power. Perhaps if more of them could have witnessed the eruption from our vantage, some of their anxieties concerning their safety could have been abated by a greater understanding of the mountain they have made their home."

Daniel Saltman and Toni Stanich flew over the vents both in daylight and after dark. Their night-time photographs are spectacular.

Left- Two geologists anxiously wait for a ride to the top of the mountain to see the Mauna Loa vents.

MAUNA LOA FROM THE VENT

The daily commute to the eruption of Mauna Loa for scientists started at a small ball field at Kilauea Military Camp. On Monday, April 2, the commuters from the Hawaiian Volcano Observatory (HVO) and the University of Hawai'i wore flame resistant jump suits, gloves, sunglasses, and backpacks containing gas masks. A chopping sound precedes the arrival of the Mauna Loa Express, a Hughes 500 helicopter skimming in over the low trees. The pilot sits in one of the two seats next to one passenger. The other two passengers go to the back of the bus where things are simpler–a plywood floor with two seat belts. The doors have been removed, so everyone checks his seatbelt carefully, and the pilot eases the helicopter into the air for another 10-minute flight to the vent. A chilly, 30-mile per hour trade wind blasts through the open door and shakes the helicopter from side to side. The passengers shout or use hand signals as their express climbs noisily up the side of the volcano. At the 9,400-foot level, the pilot carefully flies between a line of steam vents and the main fountaining vent. For a moment, sulfurous fumes fill the cockpit before the helicopter banks and lands upwind of the vent. The scientists have now arrived at work, where they will collect rock samples and measure tilt, gravity, seismicity, lava temperature, and flow rate. A low rumble can be heard coming from inside the vent as globs of molten red lava are thrown into the air and spatter, raining hot rock on the 40-foot vent ramparts.

Only a faint rushing sound can be heard as a million and a half cubic meters of lava pour out of the vent every hour, ten times the typical flow rates from Kilauea's east rift zone. The light, frothy lava rushes down Mauna Loa at 20 miles per hour, degassing and piling up against islands in the stream. As the lava piles up, it rolls back on itself in folds that look like wet cement. The river forms standing waves that are up to 12 feet high from trough to crest. There are several lava tubes within a quarter mile of the vent. One is about 10 feet across and is half-filled with a glowing lava stream. Fortunately for Hilo, few tubes have formed during this eruption. During the 1881 eruption, lava flowed rapidly and efficiently in underground tubes, insulated from heat loss, 48 kilometers down to the lowland where the city of Hilo is now located.

Blocks of dark, solid rock float in the bright red current. The density of the molten lava is so high that it is tempting to contemplate a ride downstream on the rafts of hardened lava. As the rafting blocks tumble over lava falls, however, they break up and melt in the scorching 1140° C lava river. As the lava flows 16 miles downstream, it degasses and cools, becoming denser, slower, and more viscous.

The helicopter pilot and the scientists have been watching the weather carefully. Fortunately the skies are clear, permitting a full day of work. The HVO scientists believe that the conditions near the vent are too dangerous to use a permanent camp since wind direction changes could blow the gas toward the camp or a new flow developing during bad weather could prove disastrous because nighttime helicopter evacuation could be dangerous or impossible.

As the sun descends into the volcanic haze, accentuating the reds and oranges on the mountain, the helicopter returns to carry the last three passengers on the cold, windy, 10-minute commute back to their landing field. The exhausted scientists share observations and prepare reports back at HVO, and the pilot gets some needed food and sleep. The vent fountaining reddens the evening sky over one of the largest mountain in the Pacific.

Above- In this photograph of the Mauna Loa vent system there are actually several geologists working in the foreground. However, it is difficult to spot them on the gray-black terrain. One geologist seen at mid-slope, to the left of the picture, gives an impression of the scale of these spatter ramparts.

Following page, left - Lava splatters inside the Mauna Loa vent high on the flanks of the volcano, producing a series of cinder cones.

MAUNA LOA - A VIEW FROM THE GROUND

By the morning of March 31, 1984, a group of nine Hawai'i Institute of Geophysics faculty and staff members were granted permission by civil defense administrators and prison officials to go through the Kulani Correctional Facility grounds to observe the Mauna Loa eruption. The purpose of the expedition was to get some first-hand information on some of the basic parameters of these types of low-viscosity lava flows as well as an active Moana Loa lava

flow (for many it was a first). Some of the variables that individuals were able to estimate were distance to the active vent (approximately 12.4 miles), slope of ground (approximately 4 degrees), width of the flow (20 to 33 feet), depth of flow (3-6 feet), and flow velocity in the channel (approximately 12 to 13 feet/second). These measurements are locally variable depending on distance to the vent.

The group was fortunate to be able to drive right up to the flow where it had crossed an old access road, as the only other way to get near the flows was by helicopter or flybys on small aircraft charter flights. "We stopped our vehicle at about the 6,000 foot level, where the present lava levee had knocked over electrical power lines and bisected the road. We could drive no further, nor would we have wanted to, since the active lava river was only 328 to 492 feet on the opposite side of this 3-10 foot-high levee." The active lava flow was covering the remains of an older flow, from the Mauna Loa 1942 eruption. One member of the party suggested that we park all vehicles in a ready position for a quick evacuation, because the eruptions on Mauna Loa were known to, at times, overflow the levee, forming new flow fronts as described by Macdonald (1972).

We were able to walk on top of the hardened and moderately cooled crust of an earlier overflow related to this same eruption—*moderately cooled* because it was still hot enough to melt a plastic protractor and burn cookies that were mistakenly set down on the crumbly and shelly flow. Student Mike Knight reports, "I could smell burning rubber from my thick-soled boots as I stood in awe of this spectacular sight." As the group got to within several meters of the lava river, the heat was overwhelming—too hot to allow them to directly face the flow. The heat seemed to come in waves related to thermal convection updrafts carried by small gusts of wind blowing over the lava surface. At times vision was impaired by these heat waves, which were similar to those one sees when driving in the desert on a hot summer afternoon, but more intensified. The sound of the lava river is hard to describe. "Generally, it was quiet, although a distinct sound could be heard, something like a moderately swift stream flowing over a gravel riverbed. This relatively fast-moving lava river was carrying many large blocks of solidified to crusted-over incandescent pieces of the levee

Far left- Students and faculty of the University of Hawaii saw the Mauna Loa flows from warm viewpoints along its path near Kulani Correctional Facility. Standing (from left to right): Mike Knight, Pow-foong Fan, Barry Lienert, George Walker, Elizabeth Zbinden, and Charles Helsley; Seated (left to right), Fred Duennebier, Jim Kellogg, and Barbara Keating.

Preceding page- Lava erupts from a small vent at the Mauna Loa eruption site. A pahoehoe lava flow can be seen directly in front of the vent.

wall and vent material, some as large as a small compact car (approximately 8 feet in length). We could see these larger blocks rotating and bouncing off the floor of the lava channel as they floated by. From the observations, the channel seemed to be relatively shallow, 3-7 feet deep, at this locality. At the base of small lava falls, standing waves formed the lava channel (up to 4 feet high)."

The members of the group found they experienced an eerie feeling as they stumbled over crumbly aa crust and could look down through cracks to see glowing incandescent lava just inches below the surface. At one point the top of the levee containing the lava flow began to glow orange and it appeared the lava would overflow the channel. The ground cracked beneath their feet, warning it was time to retreat a bit farther back from this vantage point. Slowly, a small tongue of lava spewed out of the side of the levee wall.

Right- This is truly a hot and uncomfortable position to be in. From this viewpoint, two lava falls can be seen in the background, with a large cooled lava raft in the middle of one lava stream. The lava stream can be seen diverting around an obstacle to flow, creating temporarily two lava flows.

Mark Twain

Mark Twain's *Letters from Hawaii* is highly recommended reading for anyone who plans to travel around the island of Hawai'i. Among the many events he witnessed and reported to newspaper readers in California was an eruption of Kilauea. He vividly pictures a summit eruption for his readers. This is an excerpt from one of his stories.

"I could see the North Lake lying out on the black floor away off in the outer edge of our panorama, and knitted to it by a web work of lava streams. In its individual capacity it looked very little more respectable than a schoolhouse on fire. True, it was about nine hundred feet long and two or three hundred feet wide, but then, under the present circumstances, it necessarily appeared rather insignificant, and besides it was so distant from us. We heard a week ago that the volcano was getting on a heavier spree than it had indulged in for many years, and I am glad we arrived just at the right moment to see it under full blast."

"Here and there were gleaming holes twenty feet in diameter broken in the dark crust, and in them the melted lava- the color a dazzling white just tinged with yellow—was boiling and surging furiously; and from these holes branched numberless bright torrents in many directions, like the "spokes" of a lady's fan, and kept a tolerably straight course for awhile and then swept round in huge rainbow curves, or made a long succession of sharp worm-fence angles, which looked precisely like the firecrest jagged lightning. These streams met other

Above- Volcanologist George Walker displays the remains of a plastic compass which was stored in his backpack as he hiked along the levee of the Mauna Loa lava stream. He briefly left his pack on a rock only to find his compass melted and his snack of crackers toasted!

Right- This photograph of the lava river shows a floating lava raft at the center of the stream. Although the photograph "freezes" the motion, the lava is actually moving with the speed of a flooded river. Rocks thrown into the flow do not skip or splash. They simply become welded to the surface and are immediately carried away. Portions of the photograph appears to be blurred because of the extreme heat coming from the very hot rocks.

streams, and they mingled with and crossed and recrossed each other in every conceivable direction, like skate tracks on a popular skating ground. Sometimes streams twenty or thirty feet wide flowed from the holes to some distance without dividing—and through the opera glasses we could see that they ran down small, steep hills and were genuine cataracts of fire, white at their source, but soon cooling and turning to the richest red, grained with alternate lines of black and gold. Every now and then masses of the dark crust broke away and floated slowly down these streams like rafts down a river. Occasionally the molten lava flowing under the superincumbent crust broke through—split a dazzling streak, from five hundred to a thousand feet long, like a sudden flash of lightning, and then acre after acre of the cold lava parted into fragments, turned up edgewise like cakes of ice when a great river breaks up, plunged downward and were swallowed in the crimson caldron. Then the wide expanse of the "thaw" maintained a ruddy glow for a while, but shortly cooled and became black and level again. During a "thaw," every dismembered cake was marked by a glittering white border which was superbly shaded inwards by aurora-borealis rays, which were a flaming yellow where they joined the white border, and from thence toward their points ta-

Left- This site is familiar to most visitors to Volcanoes National Park. During twilight hours the Kilauea inter-crater, Halema'uma'u, appears to steam as water vaporizes on the hot rock around the crater.

pered into glowing crimson, then into a rich, pale carmine, and finally into a faint blush that held its own a moment and then dimmed and turned black. Some of the streams preferred to mingle together in a tangle of fantastic circles, and then they looked something like the confusion of ropes one sees on a ship's deck when she had just taken in sail and dropped anchor–provided one can imagine those ropes of fire. Through the glasses, the fountains scattered about looked very beautiful. They boiled, and coughed, and spluttered, and discharged sprays of stringy red fire–of about the consistency of mush, for instance–from ten to fifteen feet into the air, along with a shower of brilliant white sparks–a quaint and unnatural mingling of gouts of blood and snowflakes! We left the lookout house at ten o'clock in a half-cooked condition, because of the heat from Pele's furnaces, and wrapping up in blankets (for the night was cold) returned to the hotel. After we got out in the dark we had another fine spectacle. A colossal column of cloud towered to a great height in the air immediately above the crater, and the outer swell of every one of its vast folds was dyed with a rich crimson luster, which was subdued to a pale rose tint in the depressions between. It glowed like

Right- This 1979 photograph of the Pauahi eruption shows lava erupting and cascading down the sides of the pit crater between the summit and southwest rift zone of Kilauea. The view in this photograph is remarkably similar to the views described by Mark Twain.

29

a muffled torch and stretched upward to a dizzy height toward the zenith. I thought it just possible that its like had not been seen since the children of Israel wandered on their long march through the desert so many centuries ago over a path illuminated by the mysterious "pillar of fire." And I was sure that I now had a vivid conception of what the majestic "pillar of fire" was like, which almost amounted to a revelation.

Left- Within 100-150 feet of the breached side of the Pu'u O cone, deep cracks occur in previous flows. The intense heat and steam from the rocks below precipitate sulfur and sulfur components on the rock filling the air with the smell of rotten eggs. The intense heat from this lava teepee made it uncomfortable to approach.

KILAUEA

In contrast to Mauna Loa, Kilauea volcano is quite small. The drive to the summit from Hilo is up a steady and gradual but barely perceptible slope so that it comes as a real surprise when one suddenly reaches the crater rim with its spectacular scenery. Kilauea volcano is truly a drive-in volcano. The roads in the National Park allow the visitor to drive right up to the crater rim and view the activity in safety. Footpaths allow one to hike across the crater floor.

Kilauea is probably the most active volcano in the world, although some people would give this title to the active volcano on Reunion Island in the Indian Ocean. Kilauea volcanism is not often destructive. Thus, geologists sometimes have a close view of the volcano in action. In recent years, the activity has been concentrated on the southeast rift zone. Earlier in this century, the volcanic activity centered on the summit crater.

The geological significance of these rift zone eruptions is included in the discussion of geothermal energy later in this book. Briefly, two types of eruption are typical on Kilauea. These are summit eruptions within the crater and flank eruptions outside the crater rim. The flank eruptions concentrate in the rift zone, an area of tension where the volcano is pulled apart by the force of gravity. Rift zones thus act as a path of least resistance and are often the sites of events in which molten lava moves in the subsurface but doesn't make its way to the surface (intrusive activity) as well as erup-

tions (extrusive activity). The pattern of intrusive and extrusive activity varies with time. Major earthquakes disrupt the internal plumbing of Kilauea volcano and intrusive events become common as the magma finds new pathways to the surface. After prolonged intrusive activity, conduits become established and greater volumes of magma make their way upward. Eventually, eruptive activity again becomes common.

In the recent set of eruptions, activity on the east rift zone began January 3, 1983 along a fissure or crack in the surface of the ground in the rift zone. The actual eruption was preceded by almost 24 hours of harmonic tremors detected on Hawaiian Volcano Observatory seismometers. The "harmonic tremors" are almost continual small earthquakes, a rhythmic shaking of the ground, that are associated with the movement of magma underground. Small earthquakes also occur, for as the magma ascends it must fracture and break rocks in order to force its way to the surface.

Once the magma has made its way to the surface, eruptions occur along the long crack as a line of almost continuous fountains. With time, a few of these vents become plugged and others become more pronounced. In the early phases of the recent eruption, activity was confined to two cones. First, it produced a cone approximately 350 feet high. Later it shifted to the second cone to the west. Each of these cones became a new volcanic feature formed where only flat lava flows existed before. Thus, few of these cones have official names. When activity began at the site of the first cone it

was 1123 AM–thus the name "1123 vent" has been used. When activity began at the new vent to the west, geologists began calling it the "O-vent" since it was situated at the letter "O" on the topographic maps used for outlining the extent of previous lava flows. Quite unintentionally the name Pu'u O developed, which in the Hawaiian language means "enduring hill." Because this designation has proved so appropriate, it is now commonly used and will be suggested as the official name.

Older, but of similar nature to the Pu'u O crater, is Mauna Ulu. Mauna Ulu is situated between the summit crater and Pu'u O westward along the southeast rift zone from Pu'u O. The location of the present 360-foot high mountain was not flat-flying lava flows like Pu'u O but two deep pits (300-500 feet). The eruptive activity that built Mauna Ulu began in 1969 and continued until 1974. Flows from this eruption covered portions of the Chain of Craters Road, which remained closed for years afterward. The flows entered the ocean; photographs of the hot lava entering the sea are among the most spectacular pictures of volcanic activity in the world.

Scuba-diving scientists from the University of Hawai'i took undersea photographs and movies of the lava as it entered the ocean. Because of the rapid cooling of the lava, glassy crusts formed on the surface and the lava cooled to form a pillow. Because the interior rock was still hot and moving, it would break through the crust and a new pillow-shaped lobe (1 to 2 feet in diameter) formed. Each pillow thus gave rise to one or two other pillows, until

REAL VOLCANIC HAZARD

The Volcano Golf Course, one of the most scenic courses in the world, features one of the most unusual hazards a golfer is likely to face. Not the normal man-made sand trap or pool of water, it is the result of nature at work. On the 18th hole, earthquakes have opened a crack 20 feet in length and one foot in width. According to a *Honolulu Advertiser* sports report, the superintendent of the Volcano Golf and Country Club is reported as saying, It has no apparent bottom...You drop a shot in there and that's a lost ball."

GOLFER'S BEWARE

Left- This is not the earth crack at the Volcano Golf Course. It is a much larger one near the southeast rift zone of Kilauea. Cracks like this run over a mile in length and approximately 3 feet across at the surface.

thick piles of pillow lavas formed. These movies have proven to be classic footage of undersea pillow basalt formation.

Within the summit area of Kilauea, volcanic activity varies considerably. Kilauea crater is over 3.1 miles long and 1.8 miles wide. It is approximately 350 feet deep just to the west of Volcano House Hotel and shallows to only a few feet on the western end. It is bounded by steep cliffs, or a series of benches, which step down the side of the crater. The inner crater (Halema'uma'u), technically known as a pit crater because its rim does not rise above the ground level around it, is bounded by a abrupt fault scarp. The collapsed floor of the pit lies 140 feet below the surrounding surface. Halema'uma'u stands directly above the main underground conduit through which magma rises into Kilauea volcano. During the Pu'u O eruptions the floor of the summit caldera deflated about 20 inches. Lava flows blanket the floor of Kilauea crater and range in age from 1889 to 1982. The largest of the flows occurred in 1974, 1921, and 1919.

Between the years of 1823 and 1890, Halema'uma'u contained active lava lakes that repeatedly filled, overflowed, and drained away. About 1905 (according to Richter and others, 1962), a single crater began to appear as a

long-term feature. For twenty years, this "fire pit" had a liquid convecting lava lake. Between January and March of 1924, the level of the lake dropped 279 feet. In April of that year a strong earthquake swarm took place in the Puna district and the summit deflated an additional 279 feet. This activity was associated with intrusion of magma into the southeast rift zone. The walls of Halema'uma'u collapsed at many places, covering the floor with rock rubble. Groundwater vaporized after contact with the hot rock and caused steam explosions and blasted debris from the crater for two weeks. East of the Halema'uma'u parking lot, one block weighing eight tons was thrown from the crater. An observer was struck and killed by one falling block. When the eruption ended the floor was at a depth of 1,345 feet.

Because of accumulations of lava, collapses have occurred since that time, and the crater is now partially filled. The lava covering most of the floor of Halema'uma'u crater and the eastern half of the main Kilauea crater was erupted in 1974.

During 1982 a short-lived eruption in Halema'uma'u and Kilauea crater was a delight for geologists and residents. Residents of Hawai'i came to the rim of the volcano to watch and enjoy the volcano much as they would a Friday night high school football game. There were lawn chairs, beach blankets, and coolers full of food and drink. Children ran around making new friends and having a great time, as on any other picnic. Everyone was friendly and thoroughly enjoyed the view from the rim of the crater.

At the same time, geologists from the Volcano Observatory and from the University took measurements and made observations on the floor of the crater. They hiked into the eruption from the parking lot on the downwind side of the eruption. The sulfur-rich gases coming from the eruption were extremely thick. Face masks proved a necessity during the brief walk. The geologists then observed the fountaining and lava flows from an upwind position. Throughout the afternoon and evening the fountaining shifted laterally along a fissure.

Geologist Barbara Keating relates that "one of the strangest experiences in the world is to find yourself standing on what appears to be a solid rock and have the rock gently rock and rotate beneath your feet, only to look down and see orange molten rock oozing out below what had been a solid black mass of rock!"

The most spectacular eruption in recent years was the Pu'u Pua'i eruption of 1959 on the edge of Kilauea Iki crater. This eruption was greatly enjoyed by visitors to the park because they could sit for hours in comfort and safety and watch. Several people commented that it was impossible not to collect samples of wind-spun glass called Pele's hair and Pele's tears, as they were carried by winds for great distances. The thin Pele's hair would land on clothing and break into tiny fibers.

The 1959 eruption started with a wall of lava fountains issuing from a fissure. The fountaining then localized to one vent on the fissure; sixteen phases of eruptions ensued, with repeated fountaining followed by drain-back of lava into the vent. Cinders from the eruptive activity were blown by tradewinds into the nearby forest, stripping and burying vegetation as much as 2.5 miles from the vent. A pumice hill was formed 394 feet high which was given the name Pu'u Pua'i or Fountain Hill. The crater road leads to Devastation Trail where one can hike through this partially buried forest. Trees once burned or scorched are now thriving again. A great lake of lava formed over the floor of Kilauea Iki pit crater, and where this lava lake is deepest it is believed the lava below the solid crust is still in a molten state. Drilling of the lava lake by scientists from Sandia Laboratories reached molten lava.

Kilauea, as one of the world's most active volcanoes, presents a spectrum of natural hazards (lava flows, earthquakes, tidal waves and rock falls). Each of these presents some danger to the people living near the volcano. These forces of nature will continue to build Kilauea for tens of thousands of years. Renewed activity could reactivate the volcano up to four million years later. In the meantime, residents of Hawai'i watch as their island grows.

Next pages, left- Lava from one of the Mauna Loa vents fountains into the air. The lava created by the fountaining cools quickly and a black crust forms while the lava is falling through the air.

Next Pages, right- Many Kilauea eruptions begin with a "curtain of fire" like the one shown here. As eruptive activity continues it often localizes at a single site and forms a cone.

Following page, left- A doctor's eye view of the inflamed throat of a volcano. Between volcanic eruptions the lava in the throat of the Pu'u'O crater repeatedly rose and fell within the narrow neck.

Following page, right- Two lava flows are fed in the foreground of this photograph taken of the Pu'u'O vent from a helicopter. Fountains of lava reached 225 feet above the ground during this phase of the eruption on July 23, 1983.

Preceding pages, left- Lava from the Mauna Ulu eruption (1973) flows like molten metal on the black sand beaches of Hawaii.

Preceding page, right- After 47 episodes of activity in Pu'u'O crater fissures opened in the lava fields outside the crater. Eruptive activity eventually centered on a site near Pu'u'O where a lava pond formed and became the site of continuing activity.

Right- During phase 12, geology student Mary Caress took this photograph of lava flowing out of the breach in the wall of Pu'u'o crater and splashing against the walls of the lava channel. The molten rock is obviously very fluid as it rises and spills out of the main crater's pool of lava. It is difficult to imagine that this fluid solidifies to form solid rock.

Top right- A glowing hot lava flow moves over a cinder-covered surface on April 1, 1983. Although the surface of the flow has cooled and is now black and hardened, geologist Lisa Petersen found it very uncomfortable walking on this flow. She said after a few minutes she looked down at the soles of her boots. One sole was half gone. She looked at the other boot. The sole from that boot was already gone. It had melted off!

Bottom right- The 1979 eruption of Kilauea poured over the Chain of Craters Road.

KILAUEA FROM THE GROUND

The weather is not always agreeable during a Kilauea eruption, so it often is difficult to make observations from the air. When the weather is clear, aerial photography can be used quickly and reliably to determine the extent of lava flows. Sometimes, however, ground observers need to determine the thickness of lava flows by conducting a conventional ground survey. Such was the case for geologists Chuck Helsley and Barbara Keating who, with the help of a professional surveyor, used standard surveying techniques to determine the height and position of recent lava flows.

Despite heavy rain showers, the two were flown to the Pu'u O site and were dropped on the lava flow near the breach in the volcanic cone and channel of the latest flow. The hikes across the lava flows were like hikes over mountains of broken glass. Near the vent the pahoehoe flows are fragile and glassy; often a layer of only one or two inches forms a crust over similar underlying flows. As the two scientists, acting as rodmen for the surveyor, made their way across the flows, the pahoehoe lava would crush under their feet. They could not predict whether each step might crunch into the surface a few inches or, more often, one and a half feet. When the two rodmen were not crush-

Left- Lavas from the 1971 eruption of Mauna Ulu flow into the sea forming turbulent clouds of steam at the surface and pillow lavas and volcaniclastic debris under the sea.

42

ing through the smoother pahoehoe flows, they were tramping through fragmented aa flows.

The aa flows are mounds of boulders varying in size from roughly six inches to four feet in diameter, jumbled together in a random mix. These irregularly shaped boulders are invariably so sharp they cut the skin like welded razor blades. Rather than crushing downward, these rocks roll and break in every conceivable fashion, sending the hiker in various directions, more stumbling than walking.

After a long day of surveying, the trio spent the night camped in one of two tool sheds moved to the site by Hawaiian Volcano Observatory personnel. From their sleeping bags, they could watch the pulsations of the volcano. During the night, the orange pulse of the lava moving in the throat of the volcano was visible. A bright orange glow could be seen from inside the vent, then the color dimmed to a very faint orange color against the gray-black sky. These pulsations occurred every 75 seconds. Occasionally, flashes of white light were seen in the vent. But no sound but the wind was heard and no orange, glowing rocks were flung from the vent. After an uneasy night, the trio resumed their work at dawn.

Right- Molten rock is thrown into the air from the neck of Pu'u 'O vent. The ejected rock adds material to the spatter ramparts around the vent, and helps build the cone around the active vent.

At times throughout the day, thunder could be heard, but the sound did not appear to be an effect of lightning. The white flashes and thunder might result from hydrogen gas explosions associated with gases released from the volcano. Distinct gas clouds could be seen venting from the crater; occasionally a gas cloud would turn a deep blue color from sulfur-rich gases. Only locally at cracks in the flow near the base of the cone was sulfur obvious. There sulfur compounds precipitated on the rocks, and the smell of sulfur was overpowering. The rocks were hot, and the air above cracks, often 10 to 20 feet deep, was uncomfortably hot, much like heat coming from a blast furnace. Away from these cracks, the air and rocks quickly cooled.

Right- The strength and height of volcanic fountaining is obvious in this photograph taken at Pu'u 'O crater during sunset and the evening of January 21, 1984. At the height of activity fountains reached 100-150 feet during this eruptive phase.

Left- Mark Twain would surely call this picture of Pu'u 'O "a vision of hell." The rain falling on the hot rocks surrounding the vent forms steam in this photograph of the Pu'u 'O vent taken between Phases 17 and 18 during April, 1984.

Repeatedly through the day, rain showers fell, driven by a wind so strong that the drops never fell vertically. Within thirty minutes of the first rain shower all clothing, even under rain jackets, was thoroughly soaked. Boots and work gloves filled with rain water. When the rain fell on the rocks, steam rose from every rock. Often surveying stopped because there was no visibility. On a few occasions, the rodmen found cover from the rain in lean-to's formed naturally of slabs of pahoehoe rock. More often all that was possible was to sit and wait with back to the wind and rain, surrounded by hot rocks and steam.

What a strange sight to see! This steaming volcanic terrain, so desolate. Mark Twain once described Kilauea's summit crater as "the vision of hell." One has to wonder what he would have said and written faced with this steaming version of hell only days old.

Left- Molten lava is thrown into the air at the site of a small cinder cone during the Mauna Loa eruption. The splatters of lava cool as they fall through the air producing volcanic bombs which often litter the flanks of a cone. The smooth lava at the base of the cone is called pahoehoe.

CHRONOLOGY OF KILAUEA ERUPTIONS

Phase	Date	Height of Eruption	Phase	Date	Height of Eruption
1	January–January 23, 1983	80-100 m	25	November 2–November 2	355 m
2	February 25–March 4	40-80 m	26	November 20–November 20	295 m
3	March 28–April 9	150 m	27	December 3–December 4	180-250 m
4	June 13–June 17	20 m	28	January 3–January 4, 1985	460 m
5	June 29–July 3	30 m	29	February 4–February 5	445 m
6	July 22–July 25	50-150 m	30	March 13–March 14	340 m
7	August 15–August 17	50-200 m	31	April 21–April 22	385 m
8	September 6–September 7	100-200 m	32	June 12–June 13	268 m
9	September 15–September 17	300 m	33	July 6–July 7	370 m
10	October 5–October 7	10-40 m	34	July 26–July 26	244 m
11	November 6–November 7	80 m	35	July 27–August 12	5-8 m
12	November 30–December 1	50 m	36	September 2–September 2	120-315 m
13	January 20–January 22, 1984	40 m	37	September 24–September 25	10-250 m
14	January 30–January 31	150-200 m	38	October 21–October 21	100-295 m
15	February 14–February 15	200 m	39	November 13–November 14	415 m
16	March 3–March 4	20-40 m	40	January 1–January 2, 1986	240 m
17	March 30–March 31	300 m	41	January 27–January 28	250 m
18	May 16–May 18	30-100 m	42	February 22–February 23	110-460 m
19	June 7–June 8	300 m	43	March 22–March 22	308 m
20	June 30–June 30	390 m	44	April 13–April 14	100-450 m
21	July 8–July 9	60-90 m	45	May 7–May 8	10-200 m
22	July 28–July 29	200-305 m	46	June 2–June 2	200 m
23	August 19–August 20	110-180 m	47	June 26–June 26	224 m
24	September 19–September 20	460 m			

Phase 48-During July 1986 a fissure opened roughly 3 miles northeast of Pu'u'O and lava flows from the fissure extended southeastward toward the Puna coastline. Low level eruptive activity continued along the fissure zone which resulted in numerous lava flows which moved southeastward through Royal Gardens Estate. By September 1986, the continuous eruption had built a leveed lava lake (approximately 1 mile in diameter) and shield. Low-level volcanic activity remained centered on the lava lake for many months and for the first time in many years lava flows reached the ocean.

THE VIEW FROM THE TOP

Astronomers working at the University of Hawai'i Observatory on the summit of Mauna Kea had spectacular views of the Mauna Loa flows moving downslope toward Hilo. The wind conditions remained favorable and they were able to continue their telescope work throughout much of the eruption of Mauna Loa.

During breaks from their astronomical work, Bill Sinton and Dale Cruikshank used a telephoto lens to get beautiful photographs of the distant flows and the clouds that were lit by the glow of the moving lava river. They also photographed the fountaining through personal telescopes and cameras set up outside the observatory.

David Tholen took an interesting set of photographs from a different point of view. At first sight, it appears that he photographed the meteorite streaking across the sky. But, for anyone who saw the fireball, it is immediately obvious that the setting is not correct. The sky in the photographs (next page), for example, is not lit with white light. In fact, the photograph is of a manmade meteor. If you haven't guessed, it is the re-entry of the fuel

Left- Photograph of the Mauna Loa eruption taken from Hale Pohaku near the summit of Mauna Kea. The glow from the eruption is reflected in the clouds above the lava flow.

cell of the space shuttle that was orbiting over Hawaii during the eruption. The astronomers had calculated the time of passover using information about their orbit and launch time. They were then ready and waiting with cameras and tripods poised for the event.

On the morning of April 6, viewers were treated to a double spectacle. At about 5:20 a.m. HST (eighty minutes after the launch of the Space Shuttle Challenger), the shuttle's external fuel tank re-entered the atmosphere and burned up, producing a spectacular dis-

Right- Photograph of the Mauna Loa eruption showing the re-entry and break up of the space shuttle's external fuel tank. The photograph shows a multitude of individual tracks produced by the many pieces of the broken-up fuel tank. Note the different colors and looping trajectories of some of the pieces. Many of the individual tracks show the same dashed structure produced by the tumbling of the individual pieces. On the horizon, of course, is the eruption of Mauna Loa whose show, for two to three minutes, took a backseat to the fireworks in the sky. After the last pieces of the fuel tank faded from view, a glance overhead showed the shuttle Challenger streaking across the heavens in route to a rendezvous with the Solar Maximum satellite.

play. The photograph (on the preceding page) shows the pulsating brightness of the tank, a result of the tank's tumbling. When the long dimension of the tank was aligned with its direction of motion, the streamlined profile produced less friction, thus less heat and less light. When the tank was broadside to its direction of motion, more friction produced more heat and light. The dome of the United Kingdom Infrared Telescope, seen in the lower right-hand corner, was illuminated by the glow of the Mauna Loa eruption. The smaller dome is one of the University of Hawai'i's 24-inch telescopes.

Left- While the astronauts in space worked on the Solar Maximum Mission Satellite, geologists on the ground used space-age heat retardant suits to measure the temperature of lava flows. The temperature measured exceeded 1100° C.

Following page- Astronaut George D. Nelson floats in space (his white space suit is just below the Solar Maximum Mission Satellite in this photograph taken from the space shuttle). The satellite was repaired by astronauts in space. The signals from this satellite were received here in Hawaii at the Mauna Loa Observatory despite the loss of the electrical power line due to the Mauna Loa lava flow. Electricity for the Observatory was routed through alternate power lines to keep the Observatory in operation.

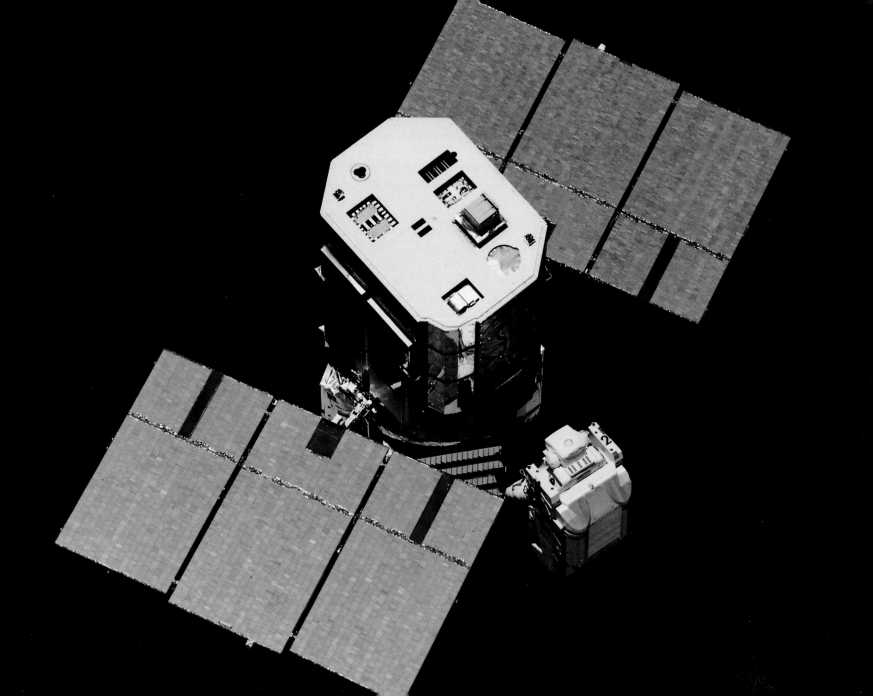

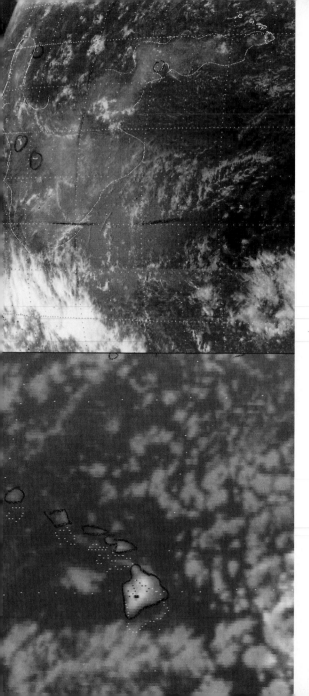

VOG

During an eruption of Kilauea or Mauna Loa it is often possible to see the effects of the eruption more than a thousand miles away. It is seen as a thick brownish cloud. Meteorologists use the term 'vog' – literally, volcanic smog. Vog comprises ash, smoke from burning vegetation, condensed water vapor, and dust. The principal chemical ingredient is sulfur dioxide (estimated at 10-20,000 tons per day at Kilauea), which oxidizes to sulfur trioxide and eventually combines with water vapor to yield sulfuric acid. The 1982 El Chichon cloud, which has persisted in the stratosphere for many years, is composed of sulfuric acid drops.

Under prevailing tradewind conditions vog can be a problem over the Big Island, especially on the Kona Coast where it becomes captured by a land breeze/sea breeze cycle. Under unfavorable meteorological conditions it can reach other islands. Typically, visibility diminishes (a hazard to aviation) and people experience

Upper left- In this satellite image, the vog (volcanic smog) extends from Hawaii westward beyond Kwajalein atoll (Marshall Islands). Note the splitting of the vog into a northward and southward branch.

Lower left- In this visible wavelength GEOS image, vog appears as an area of glare (scattered sunlight) extending southwest of the Big Island. (Time: 1645, 30 March). The volcanic activity associated with the Mauna Loa activity appears as a dark spot on the image.

eye irritation. Studies of emergency room visits and hospital admissions on O'ahu have failed to detect significant increases in respiratory distress due to vog.

Long-lived eruptions such as Mauna Loa's 1950 and 1984 flank eruptions produce vog covering large areas. In five days the Mauna Loa vog had passed Kwajalein Atoll over 2500 miles to the west and branches extended north to Wake Island and south below the equator. By 13 days after the Mauna Loa eruption the vog had reached the Philippines.

Hawaiian volcanoes also emit elemental mercury. In the 1977 Kilauea east rift eruption, mercury concentrations at Manoa on O'ahu increased to four times background values within 36 hours of the opening of the vent and persisted at that level for 15 days. Visible vog was not observed over O'ahu until late in the eruption.

Volcanic vents are generally associated with enhanced cloud activity as shown earlier. The heat ($\sim 1200°$ C) drives a buoyant plume that can trigger convective cloud formation. Cloud formation may also be enhanced by ash particles that can serve as condensation nuclei. Ash emission from Hawaiian volcanoes is not as significant as at more explosive volcanoes such as Mount St. Helens.

The adjacent photograph taken early in the Mauna Loa eruption shows the vents near the edge of the tradewind cloud layer, a deeper cloud associated with the heated air above the vents and the spread of volcanic haze as it met a stable layer near 15,000 feet above sealevel. A picture taken with a telephoto lens shows the lower tradewind cloud as a shadow. The heat at the vent was also detected by infrared satellite imagery; at 12:45 a.m. Mauna Loa and Mauna Kea appeared white (cold), but one hour later a black hotspot appeared on Mauna Loa.

In both the Kilauea and Mauna Loa eruptions, popular accounts have described anomalous precipitation near the vents (rain at Kilauea and snow at Mauna Loa). During one Kilauea phase, rain obscured the vent for an entire day, yet National Weather Service reports showed no significant rain in the surrounding Puna region. Elsewhere in the world ash-laden volcanic clouds produce spectacular lightning displays. Tornado-like vortices also frequently occur.

Upper right- A view of the Koolau range from Honolulu Harbor at 10:05 a.m., February 3, 1960. The Vog (volcanic smog) in the air is from the 1960 Kilauea flank eruption at Kapoho.

Lower right- The same view of the Koolau range from Honolulu Harbor on a clear day.

A METEORITE FIREBALL

Volcano watchers found themselves startled by an unexpected fireball streaking across the sky on March 30, 1984. Geologists from the University of Hawai'i were in the Puna district just downslope from the slow moving Phase 17 lava flow which was descending through a gulley just east of Royal Gardens subdivision. As they watched the lava, a bright light streaked across the sky, illuminating the entire landscape. Just as the light seemed to approach ground it turned a greenish color and disappeared. Students camped near Pu'u O had an even better view of the meteorite. They could clearly see a bright white ball streaking through the sky and disappearing just before reaching the ground. Mike Gaffey, a planetary geoscientist, explains that as the Big Island's two active volcanoes erupted lava to form new rock on the night of March 30, 1984, an ancient remnant from the planet's formation epoch burned up in the sky overhead. A 4.5 billion-year-old fragment of cometary debris, hitting the upper reaches of the atmosphere at a speed of about thirty kilometers per second, flared briefly into a bright fireball over the island of Hawai'i and was seen as far as O'ahu.

That at least is the most likely interpretation of the eyewitness reports of "a very bright white ball streaking through the sky with a couple of small white balls to the side" which briefly transformed night into day. Such fireballs are an uncommon phenomenon (a few hundred are reported each year and several thousand probably go unreported) produced by the high-velocity entry into our atmosphere of an asteroid or cometary fragment weighing a few kilograms. Because of the intense heat generated by friction with the tenuous gasses of the upper atmosphere, very few reach the earth's surface as anything but the finest of dust.

These tiny dust grains, collected by specially equipped aircraft flying at altitudes of 20 miles or more, provide researchers with samples of the vast regions of the solar system, as do their larger cousins the meteorites. This micrometeorite dust appears to come mostly from comets, whereas the meteorites come mostly from asteroids. In both cases, scientists are looking at material that was the very building block of the solar system.

Will fragments of the March 30 Big Island fireball find their way into the micrometeorite collections? Probably not. Usually the samples collected from high altitude contain about one micrometeorite grain for every three to five terrestrial grains (aluminum oxide spheres from solid rocket exhaust, dust from desert winds, salt crystals, and volcanic ash) collected. The recent volcanic eruption of the Mexican volcano El Chichon has increased the amount of volcanic dust high in the atmosphere by a factor of several hundred, so that the micrometeorite collecting flights have been suspended.

But was the bright light over the Big Island really a meteoric fireball? Other suggestions have been made. Traditional Hawaiian lore says that the volcano goddess, Pele, sometimes travels in her popoahi or fireball form to assert her domain. According to the April 1 issue of the *Honolulu Advertiser*, National Park Ranger Kepa Maly, a cultural expert raised in a Hawaiian family on Lana'i, explained that the snowfall atop Mauna Loa earlier in the week was interpreted by some as snow deities trying to push Pele from her mountain. The popoahi that Friday night would have been the volcano goddess reasserting her powers.

On a less traditional bent, the popoahi phenomenon may represent some type of electrical discharge like a large-scale St. Elmo's fire or like the earthquake lights reported and photographed by Chinese scientists when the earth is under great strain prior to a large earth tremor.

But whatever the explanation for the midnight lightshow, be it the more likely meteoric fireball, more esoteric electrical phenomenon, or more romantic manifestation of the Hawaiian goddess, it provided an interesting counterpoint to the flows of fire bubbling up out of the earth.

SUBMERSIBLE WAITING OFFSHORE

During Phase 17 of the Kilauea eruption, three scientists from the University of Hawai'i were conducting dives off the island of Hawai'i to investigate the submarine geology of the volcano. The project involved geologist Dave Epp, biologist David Karl, and geochemist Gary McMurtry. The three have been working on Project Pele, which is funded by the National Ocean and Atmospheric Administration (NOAA) to examine the volcanism along the submarine extension of the southwest rift zone.

The scientists made 20 dives in the University of Hawai'i submersible vessel *MAKALI'I* off the rift zone during the Phase 17 eruptions. They waited and watched, hoping the lava flow from the eruption would reach the ocean so they could have the rare opportunity to see lava flow into ocean. During the final day of Project Pele, the eruption ended and the lava flow stopped short of the sea, leaving the scientists of Project Pele very disappointed.

Right- The University of Hawaii's two-person diving vessel, the "Makali'i", is operated by the Hawaii Undersea Research Laboratory in cooperation with NOAA. The submersible allows marine scientists to study submarine features to a depth of 1,200 feet (400 meters). The scientists and submersible were off the southwest rift zone during Phase 17 activity and hoped that the flow would enter the sea. However, as often happens, the flow stopped short of the sea.

Left- Scuba diving oceanographer Richard
Grigg took this photograph of lava explosively
entering the sea during the 1971 eruption of
Mauna Ulu. When lava is extruded into the
sea it forms pillows roughly 3 feet in diameter.
The outer surface of the molten lava solidifies
and forms a crust, the interior lava then pro-
gressively bursts through the crust to form one
lobate pillow after another.

Right- Molten lava pours down the rocks of
the Puna coast as the lava reaches the ocean.
Steam clouds are produced as the rocks are
cooled by waves.

57

GEOTHERMAL RESOURCES

Geothermal power may prove to be the biggest natural asset the State of Hawai'i has. In 1985, $309,270,475 was spent in fuel costs (oil) yearly on the principal island of Oahu to generate electrical power for use by about 80 percent of the state's population. For the entire state the figure adds up to be almost one million dollars a day. This money is sent out of the state and in large part, out of the nation. Development of our geothermal resources would enable much of this money to stay here in the state of Hawai'i to provide jobs and income for the people of Hawai'i. Additionally, it would assist in decreasing the overall dependence of the United States on foreign oil.

Heat from Geothermal

The geothermal systems of Hawai'i are controlled to a large degree by the processes that form the volcanoes of the Hawaiian Islands chain. It is presently believed that thermal perturbations called hotspots melt their way through the Pacific seafloor plate to produce

Left- This view of the Geysers geothermal field in California gives an impression of the type of environmental impact the development of geothermal energy would have. The screen afforded by the Puna vegetation would significantly decrease visual impact.

58

seamounts. Islands mark the summits of many of these seamounts. Because the hotspots have persisted for many millions of years and the Pacific seafloor is moving northwestward over the hotspots, a chain of seamounts and islands is formed. The submarine extension of the Hawaiian archipelago actually reaches all the way to the Aleutians. The young end of the chain is the active seamount, Lo'ihi, just south of Hawai'i, at a water depth of 3,178 feet.

Each of the islands of Hawai'i is built of one or more volcanoes whose magma was generated deep below the Pacific seafloor (at depths of 43-68 miles. During early eruptive phases the lava extrusion rate is quite high and a roughly cylindrical conduit and magma chamber are formed near the center of the volcano. Radiating out from this conduit are usually two or three well-defined fracture systems (rift zones). As the volcano grows, the magma migrates to shallow magma chambers 1.24 to 2.5 miles beneath the summit. The rate of supply is estimated at 3,531,000 cubic feet (100,000 cubic meters) per year. From the shallow chambers it is either erupted at the summit or injected into the rift zone, where it either rises to the surface, creating a flank eruption, or remains below the surface and slowly solidifies. The formation of the rift zones is most likely a result of the pull of gravity on the massive volcanic cone. Thus, even during the process of growth, the destructive forces of gravity are at work.

Left- Rocks from the Mauna Loa aa flow glow orange as the flow slowly moved toward Hilo. The orange color atests to the heat retained in the rocks.

In recent years, summit eruptions on Kilauea volcano have been few and far between. Most of the activity has been intrusive. Thus, most of the magma supplied to the volcano has left the summit region after a brief storage period (of months or years) to travel to the southwest or east rift zone via cracks and fissures. As you can see from the photographs in this book, much of the magma makes its way to the surface, eventually forming extensive lava flows on the flanks of Kilauea. During an extrusive event, however, an estimated 1 to 25 percent of the total volume does not travel to the surface but instead stays underground as small instrusive bodies (often plate-like vertical bodies called "dikes"). These intrusive bodies are the source of the heat that composes Hawaii's geothermal resource.

Rocks that contain many fractures or vesicles formed by the release of volcanic gases during the eruptive process are highly permeable to water. Heat from surface lava flows is therefore dissipated in a short time by circulating groundwaters. The heat loss is slower where the cooling magma is surrounded or overlain by rocks of low permeability. In areas where heated groundwater is below the surface of the local water table, the weight of the overlying water can prevent this heated water at depth (3,000 to 6,000 feet) from boiling and thereby dissipating the heat. In other geothermal systems, the deeply circulating ground waters leach minerals from the rocks at depth and precipitate them in shallower zones where the temperature of the rock is cooler. The deeper hot waters can then become sealed or capped

as in a pressure cooker. Depending on the specific local environment, high-temperature geothermal systems can be found subsurface in Hawai'i. With time, even these deeply buried geothermal systems will gradually lose their heat through fumaroles and hot springs. Thus, the hotest and most active geothermal systems are found on the island of Hawaii where volcanic activity is a frequent occurrence. On the older islands of Maui, Moloka'i, Oahu and

Kauai, geothermal systems may still be present but they almost certainly are not as large or as hot as those found on Hawaii.

Use of Geothermal Energy

The abundant geothermal heat present in Hawaii was first used by early Polynesian residents of the islands for such things as bathing in warm coastal springs or for cooking food in

THE LEGEND OF 'OHI'A LEHUA

The vegetation in and around the crater of Halema'uma'u and the East Rift Zone is dominated by two plants, the delicious 'ohelo berry and the unique 'ohi'a lehua. The 'ohi'a lehua is a tree that grows with gnarled branches and bright red flowers.

Legend has it that Pele was once attracted to a handsome young Hawaiian chief named 'Ohi'a. She met him in the forest one day and told him she was a goddess and wanted him as a husband. 'Ohi'a feared that Pele would ruin his lands and people if he refused. So first he asked Pele to promise not to use her volcanic powers before he would give an answer. This she did. 'Ohi'a then refused her, saying that he was in love with the lovely Lehua. Furious, Pele turned 'Ohi'a into a twisted tree with greyish leaves. Lehua protested Pele's cruelty. Even the other gods were angered by her actions. The gods then turned Lehua into the red

blossom of the 'ohi'a tree. In this way, 'Ohi'a and Lehua could remain together always.

South and west of Halema'uma'u crater is Ka'u Desert. Mark Twain traversed a portion of this desert when traveling to see the summit eruption of Kilauea, June 3, 1866. He described it as follows; "The invincible 'ohi'a struggled for a footing even in this desert waste, and achieved it towering above the billows here and there, with trunks flattened like spears of grass in the crevices from which they sprang. We came at last to torn and ragged deserts of scorched and blistered lava–to plains and patches of dull gray ashes–to the summit of the mountain, and these tokens warned us that we were nearing the palace of the dread goddess Pele, the crater of Kilauea."

Right- The flower of the 'Ohi'a lehua tree is bright red in color and resembles a powder puff. Legend says that the 'ohi'a lehua tree is named after lovers.

the Kilauea summit fumaroles for consumption or for religous offerings. the first attempt to develop a commercial steam well in Hawaii occurred in 1962 when four shallow wells were drilled on the east rift zone of Kilauea. Even though these wells were not deep enough to produce commercial quantities of steam, some of them encountered temperatures above the boiling point of water. Since that time eleven additional geothermal exploration or research wells have been drilled on the island of Hawaii: nine were drilled on Kilauea and two more on Hualalai volcano. Although some of these recent wells have been unable to produce significant quantities of steam, all but the two wells drilled on Hualalai encountered high temperatures.

Two of the recent deep wells drilled were scientific research wells that have produced fascinating insight into the structure and hydrothermal systems of Kilauea. The first of these, a well drilled in 1973 under funding from the National Science Foundation, is located approximately 1 mile south of Halema'uma'u crater. This well was drilled to a depth of 4140 feet and reached a temperature of 135 C (275 F). Drilling was terminated in a zone of rapidly increasing temperature, indicating that much higher temperatures would have been en-

Right- With the Kilauea eruption site in view, geology students from the University of Hawaii hike cross-country to see the eruption firsthand.

countered at only slightly greater depths. The second geothermal research well was funded jointly by the state of Hawai'i and the National Science Foundation. The site for this drilling was chosen on the basis of (1) land availability in the southeast rift zone, (2) the presence of numerous shallow warm-water wells in this area, and (3) nearby geophysical anomalies detected through the use of sophisticated exploration techniques. Drilling on this well was begun in December 1975 and completed in April 1976. Testing indicated that the well was by far the hottest exploitable geothermal well ever drilled in the United States up to that time. It has a maximum bottom temperature of approximately $358°$ C ($675°$ F) and produces 45,000 kg/hr (100,000 lb/hr) of steam (55 percent) and water (45 percent). Construction of a 3-megawatt wellhead generator, sponsored by the local utility company, the county of Hawai'i, the State of Hawai'i, and the United States Department of Energy was completed in 1981. The generator facility began operation in late 1981, since that time, the generator has been able to produce power on demand for more than 90 percent of its lifetime and has very sucessfully demonstrated that the production of electrical power from Hawai'i's geother-

Left- This telephoto night time view of the Mauna Loa vents show the fiery fountains of the vent where the main lava flow originates.

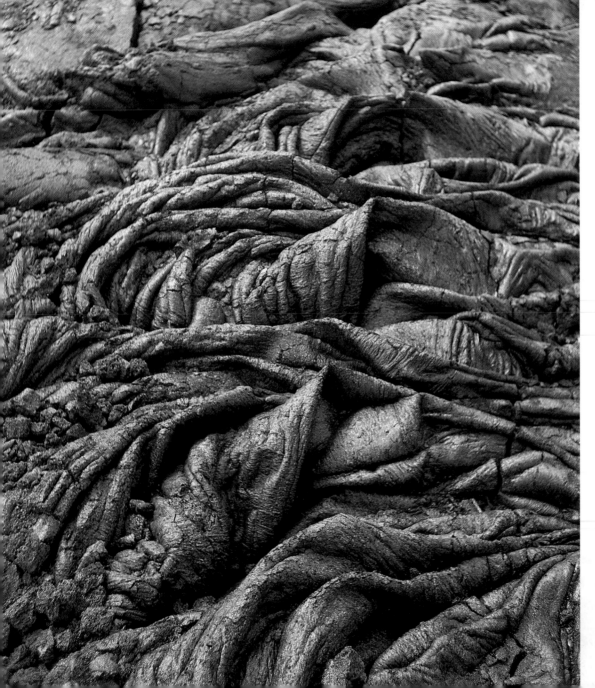

mal resources is both technically and economically feasible. This facility has also been used as a testing site for several different pollution abatement studies that have shown that hydrogen sulfide, the major pollutant from a geothermal plant, can be removed from the exhaust system of a generator facility to a value of less than two percent of the amount entering the turbine. Thus, a geothermal electrical generator, when using the technologies developed, produces less than one percent of the air pollution that an equivalent sized fossil fuel generator. The generator facility has also been recently expanded to conduct tests of secondary uses of geothermal heat for such applications as drying lumber, dying cloth, drying and cooking foodstuffs and for use in theraeutic and recreational bathing. Thus our use of geothermal heat may come full circle to include the applications that were first used by the early Polynesians.

After all is said and done, the silvery beauty of the volcanic eruption remains a constant reminder that Hawai'i continues to grow.

Left- Pahoehoe lava, which is glassy and has a low-density crust, is often iridescent silver, golden, and blue in color. As the rock ages and is weathered, this crust is worn away, leaving the denser underlying pahoehoe, which is more resistant to weathering.